بسم اللہ الرحمن الرحیم

Second Revised Edition

1418A.H./1997A.C.

الطبعة الثانية (منقحة ومزيدة)

١٤١٨هـ/١٩٩٧م

DIGEST OF
MUSLIM NAMES

Beautiful Muslim Names
and their meaning

Compiled by
Fāṭimah Suzanne Al Ja'farī

amana publications
Beltsville, Maryland, USA

amana publications
10710 Tucker Street, suite B
Beltsville, Maryland 20705-2223 USA
Tel.: (301) 595-5777 Fax: (301) 595-5888
E-mail: igamana@erols.com
Website: www.amana-publications.com

Library of Congress Cataloging-in-Publications Data

Al-Ja'fari, Fatima Suzanne 1945 (1364) -
Digest of Muslim names: beautiful Muslim names and their meaning / compiled by Fāṭimah Suzanne Al Ja'farī
p. 112 cm. 23
English and Arabic
ISBN 0-915957-68-X

1. Names, Personal--Islamic. I. Title.

CS2970. A39 1997
929.4-0917671--dc21

96-19308
CIP

التنضيد والإخراج والطباعة: مؤسسة انترناشيونال جرافيكس

Printed in the United States of America by International Graphics
10710 Tucker Street, Beltsville, Maryland 20705-2223 USA
Tel.: (301) 595-5999 Fax: (301) 595-5888 E-mail: igfx@aol.com

Contents

Male Names

Female Names

Transliteration and Pronunciation of Arabic

Accurate oral transmission is required for proper recitation of Qur‘ān and pronunciation of Muslim names. It is our duty to produce and use an accurate transliteration system which preserves the meaning. When an Arabic word is mispronounced a completely different meaning is often inferred.

Muslim names have good meanings attached to them, they are part of our identity. It becomes an individual responsibility to live up to the spirit that the name dictates. The Arabic proverb "ismun ‘alā musammā" emphasizes that through practice and self effort we earn the beautiful meaning of our name. No wonder the Prophet, Peace Be Upon-Him, made it a right of the newborn on the parents to endow him or her with an appropriate lovable name!

As Muslims of North America in particular, and of the English-speaking world in general, it is time to hold fast to our names and teach ourselves and others how to transliterate and pronounce them correctly.

Arabic possesses some unique characteristics. Unlike Latin alphabets, short vowel indicators are not part of the 28 letters of Arabic. Three of these letters (a, i, and u) are used as both consonants and vowels. When used as vowels, they are written as diacritics over or below the characters. Usually they are omitted except in Qur‘ān and primers to ensure exact rendition.

Another major difference between English and Arabic is that 9 basic sounds have non-emphatic counterparts. They are fundamentally different in echo and thickness of voice. These are: (ق ع غ ظ ط ض ص خ ح). They are produced with the back of the tongue raised toward the back of the mouth, and they are transliterated as follows: q, ‘, gh, ẓ, ṭ, ḍ, ṣ, kh, ḥ,) respectively.

The following comprehensive transliteration system is adopted. It is a complete, unambiguous and convenient system which fits the regular English softwares. When properly followed, the pronunciation will resemble the Arabic language to the best that is possible.

I. The Alphabet	**أولاً أحرف الهجاء**
1- A: long vowel (Sālim),	١- أ: ممدوده «سالم»
• A: consonant at the beginning of a word	متحركة في أول الكلمة:
A - (Aḥmad)	ـ «أحمد»
I - (Iqbāl)	ـ «إقبال»
U - (Ummah)	ـ «أمـــة»
•Ā: a vowel at the end of a word (Salmā)	ألف مقصورة «سلمى»
2- B	٢- ب
3- T	٣- ت
4- TH (thin)	٤- ث
5- J	٥- ج
6- Ḥ	٦- ح
7- KH	٧- خ
8- D	٨- د
9- DH (the)	٩- ذ
10- R	١٠- ر
11- Z	١١- ز
12- S	١٢- س
13- SH	١٣- ش
14- Ṣ	١٤- ص
15- Ḍ	١٥- ض
16- Ṭ	١٦- ط
17- Ẓ	١٧- ظ
18- ‘	١٨- ع
19- GH	١٩- غ
20- F	٢٠- ف
21- Q	٢١- ق
22- K	٢٢- ك
23- L	٢٣- ل
24- M	٢٤- م
25- N	٢٥- ن
26- H	٢٦- هـ
27- Ū- long vowel (Maḥmūd)	٢٧- واو ممدوده «محمود»

W- consonant (Nawāl)	واو متحركة (نوال)
28- Ī - long vowel (Karīm)	٢٨ – ياء ممدوده
Y - consonant (Yaḥya)	ياء متحركة (يَحْيَ)
II. *Al Hamzah*	ثانيًا– الهمزة
In the beginning of a word the same as the	في أول الكلمة:
"A" in No. 1 above in an apostrophe in the	أنظر حرف الألف رقم ١ أعلاه
middle or end of a word *(qirā'ah) (mā')*	في وسط أو نهاية الكلمة «قراءة» «ماء»
III. Vowels	ثالثًا – الحركات:
A - short vowel "*fatḥah*" *(Ḥasan)*	فتحة َ «حَسَن»
I - short vowel "kasrah" *(Bilāl)*	كسرة ِ «بِلال»
U - short vowel "*ḍammah*" *(Muḥammad)*	ضمة ُ «مُحمد»
IV. Unvowelled Consonant "*sukūn*"	رابعًا – السكون:
- *(ḥamd)*	ْ «حمْد»
V. Gemination: "*shaddah*"	خامسًا – الشدة:
- consonant doubled in pronunciation *(Razzāq)*	ّ «رزّاق»
VI. Elongation of Vowel "*madd*"	سادسًا – المدّ:
- indicates elongation of vowel *(āmīn)*	~ «آمين»
VII. Nunation- adding a vowel and an n "*tanwīn*"	سابعًا – التنوين:
an - (salāman)	ً «سلاماً»
in - (salāmin)	ٍ «سلامٍ»
un - (salāmun)	ٌ «سلامٌ»

Your Name
The Glorious Qur'ān
and Islām

by: Ismā'īl R. al Fārūqī

The title of this brief article may seem strange to the reader. What can your name possibly have to do with the Holy Book? The answer is: Rather very much, as you will see in the sequel.

If you are a Muslim, your name is in all likelihood an Arabic name, composed either of one of the names of Allah (*subḥānahu wa ta'ālā*) or of one of His divine attributes (*ṣifāt*), or of one of the names of our Prophet (*ṣalla Allahu 'alayhi wa sallam*) or one of his epithets, or the name of another prophet, or of a quality or attribute of that prophet, or of a Qur'ānic term connoting an Islamic value. It is also possible that your name be that of a *ṣaḥābī* (a companion of the prophet), or of a great Muslim of the past who has distinguished himself (herself) in the service of Islam, whether by his pen, sword, virtue, charity, statesmanship, justice, or any other Islamic value. Or, finally, it may be the very name of that value whether as a noun or an adjective.

When, in the first week of your life, you were given your name, your parents had hoped that you would grow to fulfill the Islamic value to which your name refers, to emulate the great Muslim predecessor whose name you were given. Your name must have sounded like "music" to your parents' ears; and you have grown to like it as well because it has become a part of you. Surely you want everybody to respect it, to call you by it, and to honor it by spelling it and pronouncing it correctly.

To the outside world, your name is not only a convention, i.e. a symbol denotating you. It is also a *definiens* of you, i.e. it defines you, though it may do so only partially. For instance, it certainly tells the outside world that you are a Muslim; and this is the most significant aspect of your whole being. To the attentive outsider, or to your fellow Muslim, your name also defines an aspect of Islamic history, of Islamic culture, of Islam itself. Indeed, your name is sometimes informative of Allah Himself, when it is connotative of your relationship to Him as in ‘Abdullah (‘Abd Allah), ‘Abd al Raḥmān, etc. And it may be informative of the noble Prophet whose very name you may be carrying. Respect to your name is not only respect to your own person; it is also respect to the person after whom you were named, or to the Islamic quality connoted by your name, should your name be mutilated, disrespectfully bungled or violated, all that it represents is equally violated. Juliet had wishfully thought that "by any other name a rose would smell as sweet," but found out to her sorrow that that is not true of human names. Of course persons remain the same despite changes in their names. That is not the issue. But the names themselves are often expressive of a whole history, a whole culture, a whole religion, a whole spiritual realm; and it is these which suffer through misrepresentation or misnaming.

Consider to begin with the most obvious and gravest cases. Supposing your name was Ḥāfiẓ (guardian or protector) or Ḥāmid (praiser of Allah) or Khalīq (creature). These can easily be misaccented as Ḥafīẓ, Ḥamīd or Khāliq. Immediately, your name is transformed from meaning an Islamic virtue to blasphemy. For no man may be called by a divine name. If your name was a conjunction of ‘Abd (servant) and one of the divine names, it would be equally blasphemous to mispronounce, or allow mispronunciation; e.g. ‘Abd al Ḥaqq (servant of Allah-the Truth) as Abd Al Hakk (servant of scratching). It would be an equally grave misdeed to drop ‘Abd from your name (a popular abbreviation technique used in standing by itself. If on the other hand, and for the same reason of abbreviation, the divine name is dropped, then one is left with the object Arabic name of ‘Abd, i.e., servant or slave, without specification of owner or master. In other mutilations, the divine name has been dropped, but not its demonstrative *al,* thus creating the absurd appellation, ‘Abdul or "servant of the."

Next to blasphemy stand those mispronunciations of the names of God combined with other words to make personal names, such as al Rehman instead of al Raḥmān, ‘Abd al Gafur (servant of the wide and empty) instead of ‘Abd al Ghafūr (servant of the Forgiving)' al Aliyy or Ali (the mechanical) instead of al ‘Alīy (the High). These are followed by mispronunciations or misspellings of the names of the Prophet as Munzir or Monzer (hurrier, belittler, despiser) instead of Mundhir (warner); or Muddassir (he in whom something has been plunged by force, as in assassination with a dagger) instead of Muddaththir (wrapped in his mantle, of Surah 74:1). If you object to the changing of the name of our Prophet Muḥammad to Maumet which *Webster-International* defines as "a false god or idol arising from a belief that Mohammedans worshipped images of Mohammed," "a puppet, a doll, an image, also an odd figure; a guy-often a term of abuse" and the derivative "maumetry" which the same dictionary defines as "1. idolatry, idols, and idol; 2. the appurtenances of idolatry; 3. Mohammedanism," then you ought to insist that the Prophet's name is Muḥammad, and not Mahomet, Mohamet, Mohamed, Mohamad, or Maumet.

There are of course other names which are removed from Allah and His Prophet, though they may be names of the Prophet's companions or of the great men of Islam. Such names are held in high honor and esteem by all Muslims. No Muslim should give himself or others the liberty to tamper with their spelling or pronunciation. And there are still other names which connote an Islamic meaning or value. It is offensive to the Muslim ear which comprehends those meanings and values to receive them bungled and mutilated from the hands of those who are ignorant of those meanings whether they are the carriers of these names or others.

Muslims in America are particularly prone to having their beautiful Islamic names mutilated, because of the general ignorance of Arabic or the difficulties of transliteration. Names which have a Western equivalent (Yūsuf, Ya'qūb, Ishāq,Yūnus, Mūsā, Ibrāhīm, etc.) are hastily changed into their Biblical equivalents (Joseph, Jacob, Isaac, Jonah, Moses, Abraham, etc.), without awareness that these Biblical personalities represent entirely different meanings to the Christian and/or Jew than the Qur'ānic names do to the Muslim.

If, in spite of these considerations, the Muslim in America mutilates his own name when he/she writes it in Latin characters, suffers in silence his/her name to be mutilated in writing or pronunciation by others, tolerates or encourages such mutilation, what does this tell about his/her personality?

1. Above all, it betrays his/her lax or disrespectful attitude to the names of Allah. These being Qur'ānic, his laxity is a toleration of tampering with the Qur'ānic text which is sacred. It is a defiance of Allah (*subḥānahu wa ta'ala*) since it is He who said "It is We Who

revealed the Qur'ān; and it is We Who shall safeguard it" (15:9).

2. Less grave but equally significant is the attitude of laxity or disrespect betrayed by tampering with the names of the Prophet (*ṣalla Allahu 'alayhi wa sallam*), of his companions, of the great men and women of Islam, and of Islamic meanings and values.

3. Indirectly, there is another kind of attitude betrayed in the process. It is that of tolerating the corruptions of the language of the Qur'ān by colloquial Arabic. For to pronounce or to transliterate a name in the manner it is pronounced colloquially is to tolerate colloquialism, the most dangerous and persistent threat to the language, and hence to the text of the Glorious Qur'ān. Colloquialism is the mirror of *shu'ūbīyah* and promoter of ethnocentrism. It is the beginning of resistance to the Qur'ān itself. It is not by accident that every enemy of Islam has blessed, promoted, and encouraged the colloquial dialects of the Muslim peoples. Linguists *do* know that colloquialism is the end of unity and beginning of division; and those of them that know the continuing role the Qur'ān has played in uniting us and determining our lives, *do* know that colloquialism cuts the umbilical cord which binds us to the Qur'ān.

Male Names

(خير الأسماء ما حُمِّد وعُبِّد)

(The Best of Names are those that convey Praise or Servitude to Allah)

Transliteration	Meaning	Name in Arabic
'Abd al 'Adl	Servant of The Just	عبد العَدْل
'Abd al Aḥad	Servant of The One	عبد الأحد
'Abd al 'Alī y	Servant of The Most High	عبد العليّ
'Abd al 'Aẓīm	Servant of The Great One	عبد العظيم
'Abd al 'Azīz	Servant of The Mighty	عبد العزيز
'Abd al Badī'	Servant of The Incomparable	عبد البديع
'Abd al Ba'ith	Servant of The Resurrector	عبد الباعث
'Abd al Bāqī	Servant of The Everlasting	عبد الباقي
'Abd al Bāri'	Servant of The Evolver	عبد الباري
'Abd al Barr	Servant of The Source of All Goodness	عبد البر
'Abd al Baṣīr	Servant of The All-Seeing	عبد البصير
'Abd al Bāsiṭ	Servant of The Expander	عبد الباسط
'Abd al Fattāḥ	Servant of The Opener	عبد الفتاح
'Abd al Ghaffār	Servant of The Forgiver	عبد الغفار
'Abd al Ghafūr	Servant of The Forgiving	عبد الغفور
'Abd al Ghanī	Servant of The Self-Sufficient	عبد الغني
'Abd al Hādī	Servant of The Guide	عبدالهادي
'Abd al Ḥafīẓ	Servant of The Preserver	عبد الحفيظ
'Abd al Ḥakam	Servant of The Judge	عبد الحكم
'Abd al Ḥakīm	Servant of The Wise	عبد الحكيم
'Abd al Ḥalīm	Servant of The Forebearing	عبد الحليم
'Abd al Ḥamīd	Servant of The Praiseworthy	عبد الحميد

Transliteration	Meaning	Name in Arabic
'Abd al Ḥaqq	Servant of The Truth	عبد الحق
'Abd al Ḥayy	Servant of The Living	عبد الحي
'Abd al Jabbār	Servant of The Compeller	عبد الجبار
'Abd al Jalīl	Servant of The Sublime	عبد الجليل
'Abd al Karīm	Servant of The Generous	عبد الكريم
'Abd al Khabīr	Servant of The Aware	عبدالخبير
'Abd al Khāliq	Servant of The Creator	عبد الخالق
'Abd al Laṭīf	Servant of The Subtle	عبد اللطيف
'Abd al Mājid	Servant of The Noble	عبد الماجد
'Abd al Majīd	Servant of The Most Noble	عبد المجيد
'Abd al Mālik	Servant of The Eternal Owner	عبد المالك
'Abd al Malik	Servant of The Sovereign	عبد الملك
'Abd al Matīn	Servant of The Firm One	عبد المتين
'Abd al Mu'min	Servant of The Giver of Faith	عبد المؤمن
'Abd al Mubdi'	Servant of The Originator	عبد المبدئ
'Abd al Mughnī	Servant of The Enricher	عبد المغني
'Abd al Muḥṣī	Servant of The Reckoner	عبد المحصي
'Abd al Muḥyī	Servant of The Giver of Life	عبد المحيي
'Abd al Mu'īd	Servant of The Restorer	عبد المعيد
'Abd al Mu'izz	Servant of The Honorer	عبد المعز
'Abd al Mujīb	Servant of The Responsive	عبد المجيب
'Abd al Muqaddim	Servant of The Expediter	عبد المقدم

Transliteration	Meaning	Name in Arabic
'Abd al Muqtadir	Servant of The Powerful	عبد المقتدر
'Abd al Muṣawwir	Servant of The Fashioner	عبد المصور
'Abd al Muta'āl	Servant of The Most Exalted	عبد المتعال
'Abd al Nāfi'	Servant of The Benefactor	عبد النافع
'Abd al Nūr	Servant of The Light	عبد النور
'Abd al Qādir	Servant of The Able	عبد القادر
'Abd al Qahhār	Servant of The Subduer	عبد القهار
'Abd al Qawī	Servant of The Most Strong	عبد القوي
'Abd al Qayyūm	Servant of The Self-Subsisting	عبد القيوم
'Abd al Quddūs	Servant of The Holy	عبد القدوس
'Abd al Rāfi'	Servant of The Exalter	عبد الرافع
'Abd al Raḥmān	Servant of The Beneficent	عبد الرحمن
'Abd al Raḥīm	Servant of The Merciful	عبد الرحيم
'Abd al Raqīb	Servant of The Watchful	عبد الرقيب
'Abd al Rashīd	Servant of The Righteous Guide	عبد الرشيد
'Abd al Ra'ūf	Servant of The Compassionate	عبد الرؤوف
'Abd al Razzāq	Servant of The Provider	عبد الرزاق
'Abd al Ṣabūr	Servant of The Patient	عبد الصبور
'Abd al Salām	Servant of The Peace	عبد السلام
'Abd al Ṣamad	Servant of The Eternal	عبد الصمد
'Abd al Samī'	Servant of The All-Hearing	عبد السميع
'Abd al Sattār	Servant of The Protector	عبد الستّار

TRANSLITERATION	MEANING	NAME IN ARABIC
'Abd al Shahīd	Servant of The Witness	عبد الشهيد
'Abd al Shakūr	Servant of The Appreciative	عبد الشكور
'Abd al Tawwāb	Servant of The Acceptor of Repentance	عبد التواب
'Abd al Wāḥid	Servant of The Unique	عبد الواحد
'Abd al Wadūd	Servant of The Loving	عبد الودود
'Abd al Wahhāb	Servant of The Bestower	عبد الوهاب
'Abd al Wājid	Servant of The Finder	عبد الواجد
'Abd al Wakīl	Servant of The Trustee	عبد الوكيل
'Abd al Wālī	Servant of The Governor	عبد الوالي
'Abd al Walīy	Servant of The Protecting	عبد الولي
'Abd al Wārith	Servant of The Supreme Inheritor	عبدالوارث
'Abd al Ẓāhir	Servant of The Manifest	عبد الظاهر
	* * *	
Abū Bakr	The Companion of Prophet Muhammad *(The first Caliph)*	أبو بكر
Abū al Khayr/Khair	One who does good deeds	أبو الخير
Ādam	The name of the father of humanity, *(The first man created by Allah and the first Prophet)*	آدم
Adham	Old Arabic name *(Lit.: Black or dark)*	أدهم
Adīb	Cultured, wellmannered person	أديب
Aḥmad	Commendable, praiseworthy *(One of the names of Prophet Muḥammad)*	أحمد

Transliteration	Meaning	Name in Arabic
Akram	Very generous	أكرم
Al ‘Abbās	Discription of a lion *(Name of the Prophet's uncle)*	العباس
Alḥasan	The handsome, the good, *(Name of the Prophet's grandson)*	الحسن
Alḥusayn/Alhusain	Diminutive of the handsome, the good *(Name of the Prophet's grandson)*	الحسين
Almahdī	Guided to the right path	المهدي
Alṭāf	Kindness	ألطاف
Amīn/ Al Amīn	Trustworthy, *(One of the Prophet's names)*	أمين /الأمين
Amīr	Ruler, prince, leader	أمير
Amjad	Very glorious	أمجد
Anas	Very sociable *(Name of Prophet's companion)*	أنس
Anīs	Affable, sociable	أنيس
Anwar	Radiant, *(Full of light)*	أنور
Asad	Lion	أسد
As‘ad	Happy, fortunate, lucky	أسعد
Ashraf	Most noble, honorable	أشرف
Athīr	Favored, preferred	أثير
‘Awf	Old Arabic name *(L.:A plant with a nice smell)*	عوف
Aws	Old Arabic name *(Lit.: To give)*	أوس
Awwāb	Returning *(To Allah)*	أوّاب

Transliteration	Meaning	Name in Arabic
Ayham	Old Arabic name , brave	أيهم
Ayman	On the right, fortunate	أيمن
Ayser	Easy in dealing, wealthy	أيسر
Ayyūb	A prophet's name *(Biblical Job)*	أيوب
Azhar	Shining, radiant, glowing	أزهر
Al Barā'	Wholesome with innocence	البراء
Al Ḥakam	The arbitrator, the judge	الحكم
Al Ḥārith	Old Arabic name *(Lit.: Plowman)*	الحارث
Al Ṣāfī	Clear, pure, fine	الصافي
Al Ṭayyib	The good one	الطيّب
Al Tijanī	Crowning	التيجاني
Al Ṭufayl/ Al Ṭufail	Old Arabic name	الطفيل
'Ābid	Worshipper	عابد
'Ābidīn	Worshippers, adorers	عابدين
'Ādil	Just, fair	عادل
'Adlī	Judicial, juridical	عدلي
'Adnān	Old Arabic name	عدنان
'Afīf	Chaste, modest	عفيف
'Ajīb	Wonderful	عجيب
'Ākif	Focused	عاكف
'Alā'	Nobility, excellence	علاء
'Alā' al Dīn	Excellence of faith	علاء الدين

Transliteration	Meaning	Name in Arabic
'Aliy/ 'Alī/ Ali	Excellent, noble *(Name of the Prophet's son-in-law and the fourth Caliph)*	علي
'Amīd	Support	عميد
'Āmir	Prosperous, populous	عامر
'Ammār	One who is a builder, long lived or preserver of life	عمّار
'Amro	Old Arabic name	عمرو
'Antarah	Name of an Arab folk hero *(To display hero-ism)*	عنترة
'Aqīl	An old Arabic name	عقيل
'Āṭif	Compassionate	عاطف
'Ārif	Acquainted, knowledgeable	عارف
'Āṣim	Protector	عاصم
'Aṭā'	Giving, gift	عطاء
'Aṭā'Allāh	Gift of Allāh	عطاء الله
'Aṭā' al Raḥmān	Gift of the Merciful	عطاء الرحمن
Athīl	To be firmly rooted	أثيل
'Aṭīyah	Gift	عطية
'Awaḍ	Reward, compensation	عوض
'Azab	Touring, wandering, travelling	عزب
'Azīz	Powerful (dear)	عزيز
'Azzām	Determined	عزّام

Transliteration	Meaning	Name in Arabic
Badī‘	Marvelous	بديع
Badī‘ al Zamān	The marvel of time	بديع الزمان
Badr al Dīn	Full moon of faith	بدر الدين
Badr	Full moon	بدر
Badrī	One who took part in the battle of Badr *(early)*	بدري
Bahā'	Beauty, splendor	بهاء
Bahā’ al Dīn	The magnificent in the faith	بهاء الدين
Bahīj	Cheerful	بهيج
Bāhir	Dazzling, brilliant	باهر
Bahīr	Dazzle	بهير
Bahīy al Dīn	The magnificence of the faith	بهي الدين
Bakr	Old Arabic name	بكر
Bakrī	One who starts his work early	بكري
Balīgh	Eloquent	بليغ
Bandar	Old Arabic name (*Lit.: Seaport, district capital)*	بندر
Barīr	Faithful	برير

Transliteration	Meaning	Name in Arabic
Bāsil	Brave	باسل
Bāsim	Smiling	باسم
Basīm	Smiling	بسيم
Bashīr	Bringer of glad tidings	بشير
Bashshār	Bringer of many glad tidings	بشار
Bassām	Smiling	بسام
Bayhas	Name of the lion	بَيْهس
Bilāl	The first African Muslim who became the Prophet's *mu'adhdhin (The one who calls for prayer) (Lit.: What satisfies thirst)*	بلال
Bishārah	Good tidings	بشارة
Bishr	Joy	بشر
Budayl/ Budail	Name of a companion of the Prophet	بُدَيل
Burhān	Proof	برهان
Bushr	Joy, happiness	بُشر

Transliteration	Meaning	Name in Arabic

ضياء

Dānī	Near, close	داني
Darwīsh	Dervish	درويش
Dāwūd	A Prophet's name (*Biblical David*)	داوود
Dhākir	One who remembers God frequently	ذاكر
Dhakīy	Intelligent, bright	ذكي
Dhu al Fiqār	The name of the sword of 'Alī ibn Abī Ṭālib	ذو الفقار
Dhu al Kifl	A prophet's name	ذو الكفل
Dhakwān	Intelligent	ذكوان
Durayd	Old Arabic name (*Lit.: Toothless*)	دريد
Ḍirār	Old Arabic name	ضرار
Ḍiyā'	Brightness, light	ضياء
Ḍiyā' al Dīn	Light of the faith	ضياء الدين

Transliteration	Meaning	Name in Arabic
Fādī	Redeemer	فادي
Fāḍil	Superior, honorable	فاضل
Faḍīl	Virtuous	فضيل
Faḍl	Favor, surplus	فضل
Faḍl Allah	Favor of Allāh	فضل الله
Fahd	Lynx	فهد
Fahmī	Understanding	فهمي
Fā'iz	Winner	فائز
Fākhir	Outstanding/ Pride	فاخر
Fakhrī	Honorary person (pride)	فخري
Fakhr al Dīn	Pride of the faith	فخر الدين
Falāḥ	Success	فلاح
Fāliḥ	Successful	فالح
Faraj	Relief, freedom from grief	فرج

Transliteration	Meaning	Name in Arabic
Fāris	Cavalier, horseman, knight	فارس
Farḥān	Happy	فرحان
Farīd	Rare, unique	فريد
Farīz	Classify (deriv.)	فريز
Fārūq	He who Distinguishes truth from falsehood	فاروق
Fatḥī	To do with conquest	فتحي
Fātiḥ	Conqueror	فاتح
Faṭīn	Clever, smart	فطين
Fawzān	Victorious	فوزان
Fawzī	To do with success	فوزي
Fawwāz	Always very successful	فواز
Fayṣal/ Faiṣal	Decisive, criterion, arbitrator	فيصل
Fayyāḍ	Overflowing, generous	فياض
Fidā'	Redemption, sacrifice	فداء
Fikrī	Thought & ideals (deriv.), intellectual	فكري
Firās	Perspicacity	فراس
Fu'ād	Heart	فؤاد

Transliteration	Meaning	Name in Arabic

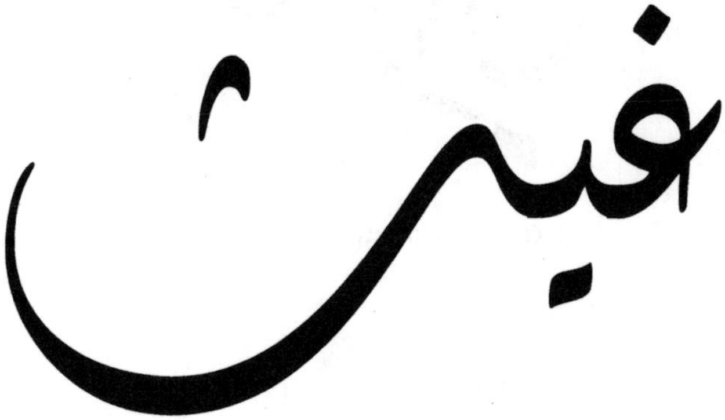

Ghālī	Valuable, dear, beloved, expensive	غالي
Ghālib	Victor	غالب
Ghānim	Successful	غانم
Ghassān	Ardor, Vigor (of youth)	غسان
Ghawth	Succor, to help	غوث
Ghāzī	Conqueror	غازي
Ghazwān	One on expedition, to conquer	غزوان
Ghayth/ Ghaith	Rain	غيث
Ghiyāth	Succorer	غياث

هادي

Transliteration	Meaning	Name in Arabic
Hāđī	Guiding to the truth	هادي
Hamīm	Zealous	هميم
Hanā'ī	Of happiness	هنائي
Hannād	An old Arabic name	هناد
Hāni'	Joyful, happy	هانیء
Hārūn	A prophet's name (*Biblical Aaron)*	هارون
Hāshim	An old Arabic name *(Name of the Prophet's great grandfather, named so for his generosity)*	هاشم
Haytham	Young hawk	هيثم
Hilāl	New moon, crescent	هلال
Hishām	Generous	هشام
Hūd	A prophet's name (*Biblical Hud*)	هود
Hudad	A name of pre-Islamic Arabian king	هُدد
Humām	Brave and noble, courageous, generous	همام
Ḥabbāb	Affable, lovable, darling	حبّاب

TRANSLITERATION	MEANING	NAME IN ARABIC
Ḥabīb	Beloved	حبيب
Ḥāfiz	Protector, One who has memorized the Qur'an	حافظ
Ḥakīm	Wise	حكيم
Ḥanīf	True believer	حنيف
Ḥamās	Enthusiasm	حماس
Ḥamdī	Of praise	حمدي
Ḥāmid	Praising (God)	حامد
Ḥamīm	Intimate, close friend	حميم
Ḥamzah	Lion *(Name of the Prophet's uncle)*	حمزة
Ḥāris	Guardian, protector	حارس
Ḥārith	Old Arabic name (*Lit.: One who plows)*	حارث
Ḥārithah	Old Arabic name *(Lit.: One who plows well)*	حارثة
Ḥasan	Good, beautiful, handsome	حسن
Ḥasīb	Noble, respected	حسيب
Ḥassān	Good doer, make things better	حسّان
Ḥātim	Judge	حاتم
Ḥāzim	Resolute	حازم
Ḥaydar	Lion	حيدر
Ḥayyān	Old Arabic name	حيان
Ḥilmī	Gentle, calm	حلمي
Ḥudhāfah	An old Arabic name	حذافة

TRANSLITERATION	MEANING	NAME IN ARABIC
Ḥudhayfah/ Ḥudaifah	Old Arabic name	حذيفة
Ḥusām	Sword	حسام
Ḥusām al Dīn	The sword of faith	حسام الدين
Ḥusayn/ Ḥusain	Beautiful, handsome, doer of good deeds	حسين
Ḥusni	Of goodness or beauty	حسني

Ibrāhīm	A prophet's name *(Biblical Abraham)*	إبراهيم
Idrīs	A prophet's name	إدريس
Ī hāb	Donation	إيهاب
Iḥsān	Kindness, doing very well, beneficence *(Highest level of Iman)*	إحسان
Iḥtishām	Modesty, decency	احتشام
Iliās	A Prophet's name *(Biblical Elijah)*	إلياس
Imām	Leader *(Of prayer or community)*	إمام

Transliteration	Meaning	Name in Arabic
Imtiyāz	(Mark of) distinction or excellence	إمتياز
In'ām	Act of benefaction, bestowal	إنعام
Iqbāl	Prosperity, good fortune	إقبال
Is-ḥāq	A prophet's name *(Biblical Isaac)*	إسحاق
Ismā'īl	A prophet's name *(Biblical Ishmael)*	إسماعيل
Iyād	Old Arabic name *(Lit.: A pigeon)*	إياد
'Īd	Feast, festival	عيد
'Ikrimah	Old Arabic name	عكرمة
'Imād	Pillar, support	عماد
'Imād al Dīn	The pillar of the faith	عماد الدين
'Imrān	Be long-lived	عمران
'Irfān	To be grateful	عرفان
'Ī sā	Prophet Jesus	عيسى
'Iṣām	Safeguard	عصام
Iyās	Consoling	إياس
'Izz al Dīn	Might of the faith	عز الدين

جعفر

Transliteration	Meaning	Name in Arabic
Jabalah	Old Arabic name *(Lit.: Mount, hill)*	جبلة
Jabr	Old Arabic name (brave)	جبر
Jābir	Consoler, comforter	جابر
Jād Allalh	Gift of God	جاد الله
Ja'far	Old Arabic name *(Lit.: Rivulet, little creek)*	جعفر
Jāl	Resolution, firm will	جال
Jalāl	Glory	جلال
Jalāl al Dīn	Glory of the faith	جلال الدين
Jalīl	Grand, exalted	جليل
Jamāl	Beauty, handsomeness	جمال
Jamāl al Dīn	Beauty of the faith	جمال الدين
Jamīl	Handsome, graceful, goodlooking, charming	جميل
Jarīr	Old Arabic name *(Lit.: One who can pull)*	جرير
	Name of a famous Arab poet	
Jāsim	Great, big, huge	جاسم

Transliteration	Meaning	Name in Arabic
Jaul	Kind of unit, choice	جَول
Jaun	*(Lit.: Antonyms, e.g. light and darkness),* kind of plant	جَون
Jawād	Generous	جواد
Jibrān	Old Arabic name	جبران
Jibrīl	The Angel Gabriel	جبريل
Jihād	Striving for the sake of God, struggle	جهاد
Jubayr/ Jubair	Old Arabic name	جبير
Jul	Mind, resolution, firm will	جول
Jumu'ah	Friday	جمعة
Junayd/ Junaid	Young fighter	جنيد
Juwayn/ Juwain	Sibling	جُوين
Jawdah/ Jawdat	Heavy rain, benevolent deed	جودة / جودت

Transliteration	Meaning	Name in Arabic

Ka‘b	Old Arabic name *(Lit.: Ankle bone)*	كعب
Kamāl	Perfection	كمال
Kāmil	Perfect	كامل
Kamīl	Perfect, complete	كميل
Karam	Generosity	كرم
Kārim	Generous	كارم
Karīm	Generous, noble	كريم
Kātib	Scribe, writer	كاتب
Kāẓim	Well - tempered, cool, patient	كاظم
Kumayl / Kumail	Diminutive of kamīl	كُمَيْل

TRANSLITERATION	MEANING	NAME IN ARABIC

Khalaf	Descendant, successor	خلف
Khaldūn	Old Arabic name *(Lit.: Eternal)*	خلدون
Khālid	Eternal	خالد
Khalīfah	Caliph, successor	خليفة
Khalīl	Friend	خليل
Khalīl al Allāh	The Friend of God *(Also the title given to Prophet Ibrāhīm)*	خليل الله
Khāliṣ	Pure, clear	خالص
Khayrī/ Khairi	Charitable, beneficent	خيري
Khayr al Allāh	The good from God	خير الله
Khayr al Dīn	The goodness of the faith	خير الدين
Khulūṣ	Clearness, purity	خلوص
Khuzaymah/Khuzaimah	Old Arabic name	خزيمة

TRANSLITERATION	MEANING	NAME IN ARABIC
Labīb	Sensible, intelligent	لبيب
Lablāb	English ivy	لبلاب
Laṭīf	Courteous, nice, gentle, delicate, polite	لطيف
Layth	Lion	ليث
Lu'ay	Shield	لؤي
Lubayd/ Lubaid	Old Arabic name	لبيد
Luqman	Name of the legendary sage/wise man in the Qur'an	لقمان
Luṭ	A prophet's name *(Biblical Lot)*	لوط
Luṭfi	Gentle, from kindness	لطفي

مهدي

TRANSLITERATION	MEANING	NAME IN ARABIC
Maḥbūb	Beloved, dear	محبوب
Ma‘bad	Place of worship, old Arabic name	معبد
Ma‘d	Old Arabic name	معد
Madanī	Urban, civilized, modern	مدني
Mahdī	Guided to the right path	مهدي
Maḥfūẓ	Protected (by God), safe	محفوظ
Māhir	Skillful	ماهر
Maḥjūb	Concealed, veiled	محجوب
Maḥmūd	Praiseworthy, praised	محمود
Mahrah	Name of an Arabian tribe	مهرة
Mahrān	Name of a river in India	مَهران
Maḥrūs	Protected *(by God)*	محروس
Majd	Glory	مجد
Majd al Dīn	Glory of the faith	مجد الدين

TRANSLITERATION	MEANING	NAME IN ARABIC
Majdī	Glorious *(Of glory)*	مجدي
Mājid	Glorious	ماجد
Majīd	Glorified	مجيد
Makīn	Well-founded, strong, firm	مكين
Mulham	Inspired	مُلهَم
Mulhim	Inspiring	مُلهِم
Mālik	Master, owner	مالك
Mamdūḥ	One who is commended *(Praised)*	ممدوح
Ma'mūn	Trustworthy, trusted	مأمون
Ma'in	Benefit *(Old Arabic name)*	مَعن
Munāhid	Strong	مُنَاهد
Mandhūr	Vowed, consecrated to God	منذور
Marghūb	Desirable, coveted	مرغوب
Ma'rūf	Well-known, good	معروف
Manṣūr	Victorious	منصور
Marzūq	Fortunate *(By God)*	مرزوق
Marwān	Old Arabic name	مروان
Mashhūr	Famous	مشهور
Masrūr	Happy, joyful	مسرور
Mas'ūd	Happy, lucky	مسعود
Maṣūn	Well-protected, sheltered	مصون
Maẓhar	Appearance	مظهر

TRANSLITERATION	MEANING	NAME IN ARABIC
Māzin	Old Arabic name	مازن
Maymūn	Lucky, fortunate	ميمون
Maysarah	Of comfort, ease	ميسرة
Mihrān	Name of a companion of the Prophet	مهران
Mihyār	Name of a famous poet	مِهيار
Mikā'īl	Name of an Angel *(Michael)*	ميكائيل
Miqdād	Old Arabic (*Name of a Ṣaḥabī)*	مقداد
Miṣbāḥ	Lamp, light	مصباح
Mish'al	Torch, light	مشعل
Miyāz	Distinguished, preferred	مياز
Mu'mmar	Given or granted long life	مُعمّر
Mu'ādh	Old Arabic name (*Name of a Companion)*	معاذ
Mu'āwiyah	*(First Umayyad Caliph)*	معاوية
Mu'ayyad	Supported *(by God)*	مؤيد
Mubārak	Blessed	مبارك
Mubīn	Clear, evident	مبين
Muḍar	An Arabian tribe *(Name of a great grandfather of the Prophet)*	مضر
Muddaththir	Covered up *(A title of Prophet Muhammad)*	مدثر
Mufīd	Useful, helpful	مفيد
Mufliḥ	Successful	مفلح
Muhāb	Dignified	مهاب

Transliteration	Meaning	Name in Arabic
Muhammad	Praised, praiseworthy	محمد
Muhannā	Happy, delighted	مهنّى
Muhannad	Sword	مهند
Muhayr/ Muhair	Old Arabic name *(Lit.: Skilled)*	مُهَيْر
Muhīb	Noble, respected	مهيب
Muḥibb	Loving	محبّ
Muḥyī al Dīn	Reviver of the religion	محيي الدين
Muḥsin	Beneficent, charitable	محسن
Muhtadī	Rightly guided	مهتدي
Muʿīn	Supporter, helper	معين
Mu'izz	Comforter	معز
Mujāb	One whose prayers were answered	مجاب
Mujāhid	One who struggles in the cause of God	مجاهد
Mukarram	Honored	مكرم
Mukhliṣ	Faithful, sincere	مخلص
Mukhtār	The chosen	مختار
Mu'min	Believer	مؤمن
Mumtāz	Excellent	ممتاز
Mundhir	Warner, cautioner	منذر
Munīb	Repentant	منيب
Munīf	Exalted, excellent	منيف
Munīr	Brilliant, shining	منير

Transliteration	Meaning	Name in Arabic
Mu'nis	Pleasant companion	مؤنس
Munjid	Helper	منجد
Munṣif	Just, right	منصف
Muntaṣir	Victorious	منتصر
Murād	Wanted, desired	مراد
Murshid	Guide	مرشد
Murtaḍā	Contented, pleased	مُرتضى
Mūsā	A prophet's name *(Biblical Moses)*	موسى
Musā'id	Helper, supporter	مساعد
Muṣ'ab	Old Arabic name	مصعب
Mus'ad	Favored by fortune, lucky	مسعد
Muṣliḥ	Conciliator, reformer	مصلح
Muslim	Submitting himself to God	مسلم
Muṣṭafā	Chosen *(One of Prophet Muhammad's names)*	مصطفى
Mushtāq	Longing, yearning	مشتاق
Muṭā'	One who is obeyed	مطاع
Mu'taṣim	Adhering *(To faith, to God)*	معتصم
Mutawallī	Entrusted	متولي
Mu'tazz	Proud, honorable	معتز
Muthanna	Old Arabic name	مثنى
Muṭī'	Obedient	مطيع
Muyassar	Fortunate, fascilitated	ميسر

Transliteration	Meaning	Name in Arabic
Muwaffaq	Successful, lucky	موفق
Muẓaffar	Victorious	مظفر
Muzzammil	One who is wrapped up *(Title of Prophet Muhammad)*	مزمل

نبيل

Nābighah	Intelligent	نابغة
Nabīh	Smart	نبيه
Nabīl	Noble, honorable	نبيل
Nadhīr	Warner	نذير
Nadīm	Friendly, entertaining	نديم
Nādir	Rare, precious	نادر
Nāfi'	Useful	نافع
Nahīd	Generosity	نهيد
Nā'il	Acquirer, earner	نائل
Na'īm	Comfort, tranquility	نعيم
Nājī	Safe, survivor	ناجي

Transliteration	Meaning	Name in Arabic
Najīb	Noble descent, outstanding	نجيب
Najīd	Lion, brave	نجيد
Najm al Dīn	The star of the faith	نجم الدين
Na'mān	Old Arabic name	نعمان
Namīr	Good, pure, dear	نمير
Nash'ah/ Nash'at	Growing up, youth	نشأة/ نشأت
Nashwān	Exultant, elated	نشوان
Nasīb	Noble, relative	نسيب
Nāṣiḥ	Advisor, counselor	ناصح
Naṣīḥ	Faithful, advisor	نصيح
Nāṣir	Helper, protector	ناصر
Naṣīr	Helper, supporter	نصير
Naṣr	Victory	نصر
Naṣrī	Of victory	نصري
Naṣūḥ	Sincere, faithful	نصوح
Nawwāf	High, tall, lofty	نواف
Nawfal	Sincere, faithful	نوفل
Nāyif	High, excellent	نايف
Nazīh	Honest, chaste	نزيه
Nāẓim	Generous (*Old Arabic name for the sea)*	ناظم
Naẓmī	Arranger, organiser	نظمي
Nibrās	Lamp, light	نبراس

Transliteration	Meaning	Name in Arabic
Niḍāl	Struggle	نضال
Nijād	Tall, dominant	نجاد
Nimr	Tiger	نمر
Nizār	Old Arabic name	نَزَار
Nu'aym/ Nu'aim	Name of several of the Prophet's companions	نُعيم
Nu'mān	An old Arabic name *(Rosy color)*	نُعمان
Nūḥ	A Prophet's name *(Biblical Noah)*	نوح
Nuhayd/ Nuhaid	Big	نُهيد
Nūr al Dīn	Light of the faith	نور الدين
Nūrī	Shining with nūr *(My nūr)*	نوري
Nuṣrah/ Nuṣrat	Help, support	نصرة / نصرت

قتيبة

Transliteration	Meaning	Name in Arabic
Qāsim	Divider	قاسم
Qatādah	Name of a companion of the Prophet	قتادة
Qays (Qais)	Old Arabic name *(Firm)*	قيس
Qudāmah	Courageous	قدامة
Quṣay	Old Arabic name	قصي
Qutaybah/Qutaibah	Old Arabic name, (Lit.: Impatient) *(Famous Muslim leader)*	قتيبة
Quṭb	Leader	قطب

رفيق

Transliteration	Meaning	Name in Arabic
Rabāḥ	Gainer, winner	رباح
Rabī‘	Spring	ربيع
Rabī‘ah	Old Arabic name	ربيعة
Rā’id	Leader	رائد
Rā’if	Merciful, gentle	رائف
Rajā’	Hope	رجاء
Rāḍī	Satisfied, content	راضي
Rāfid	Support, creek	رافد
Rāfil	Good living, luxurious	رافل
Rafīq	Companion, kind friend	رفيق
Rāghib	Willing, desirous	راغب
Raghīd	Pleasant	رغيد
Rajab	The seventh month of the Muslim lunar calendar	رجب

TRANSLITERATION	MEANING	NAME IN ARABIC
Rājī	Hoping, full of hope	راجي
Rājiḥ	Having the upper hand, more acceptable	راجح
Rakīn	Firm, confident	ركين
Ramaḍān	The ninth month of the Muslim lunar calander *(The month of fasting)*	رمضان
Rāmī	Marksman	رامي
Ramīz	Honored, respected	رميز
Rāmiḥ	Arcturus (Brightest star in Bootes, a constellation)	رامح
Rāmiz	Symbolic	رامز
Ramzī	Symbolic, in code, coded	رمزي
Rānī	Gazing, to gaze	راني
Rashād	Maturity, wisdom	رشاد
Rāshid	Having the true faith	راشد
Rashīd	Rightly guided, wise	رشيد
Rasīl	Messenger	رسيل
Raṣīn	Composed	رصين
Rasmī	Formal, official	رسمي
Rasūl	Messenger	رسول
Rātib	Regular	راتب
Ra'ūf	Merciful, gentle	رؤوف

TRANSLITERATION	MEANING	NAME IN ARABIC
Rayḥān/ Raiḥān	Aromatic plant, sweet basil	ريحان
Rayyān	Well-watered, luxuriant *(One of the gates of paradise)*	ريان
Razīn	Composed, subtle	رزين
Riḍā	Contentment, satisfaction	رضا
Riḍwān	Forgiveness, satisfaction, consent	رضوان
Riḥāb	Vastness	رحاب
Rizq	Subsistence, blessing of God	رزق
Riyāḍ	Meadows, gardens	رياض
Rūḥī	Spiritual	روحي
Rushd	Maturity, wisdom, sensible conduct	رشد
Rushdī	Mature, wise	رشدي
Ruwayd /Ruwaid	Walking gently	رويد

Transliteration	Meaning	Name in Arabic

سمير

Sa‘ādah	Happiness	سعادة
Sadād	Right thing to do, lucky hand	سداد
Sa‘d	Good luck	سعد
Sadīd	Relevant, correct, right	سديد
Sa‘d al Dīn	The good of the faith	سعد الدين
Sa‘dūn	Happy	سعدون
Sa‘īd	Happy	سعيد
Sab‘	Lion	سبع
Sā‘idah	Helping	ساعدة
Sahl	Easy to deal with	سهل
Sājid	Prostrating in adoration	ساجد
Sajjād	One who prostrates a lot	سجاد
Salamah	Having integrity, wholesome	سلمة
Salāmah	Safety	سلامة
Sālim	Safe, healthy	سالم
Salīm	Healthy	سليم

Transliteration	Meaning	Name in Arabic
Sāmī	High, elevated	سامي
Sāmiḥ	Forgiving	سامح
Samīḥ	Forgiving, liberal	سميح
Sāmir	Entertaining, companion	سامر
Samīr	Entertaining, companion	سمير
Sāriyah	A cloud raining at night *(Name of a companion of the Prophet)*	سارية
Sāṭi'	Shining, bright	ساطع
Sayf/ Saif	Sword	سيف
Sayf al Dīn	Sword of the faith	سيف الدين
Salmān	Healthy, safe, wholesome *(Name of the first Persian to embrace Islam)*	سلمان
Sayyid	Master	سيد
Sinān	A spearhead	سنان
Sirāj	Lighted torch	سراج
Sirāj al Dīn	The light of the faith	سراج الدين
Suhayl/ Suhail	Easy to deal with, canopus, *(A star in the sky)*	سهيل
Suhaym/ Suhaim	Old Arabic name *(Diminutive of arrow)*	سهيم
Sulaymān/ Sulaiman	A Prophet's name *(Biblical Solomon)*	سليمان
Sumrah	Brownness	سُمرة
Su'ūd	Good luck	سعود

TRANSLITERATION	MEANING	NAME IN ARABIC
Sufyān	Old Arabic name	سفيان
Sulṭān	Sultan, king	سلطان
Surāqah	Name of a companion of the Prophet	سُراقة

شهير

TRANSLITERATION	MEANING	NAME IN ARABIC
Sha'bān	The eighth month of the Muslim lunar calendar	شعبان
Shadī	Singer, enchanter	شادي
Shādin	Fawn, young deer	شادن
Shāfi'	Mediator	شافع
Shafī'	Mediator	شفيع
Shafīq	Kind, compassionate, tender	شفيق
Shāhid	Witness/ witnessing	شاهد
Shahīd	Martyr	شهيد
Shāhīn	Hawk	شاهين
Shahīr	Well-known, famous	شهير
Shakīb	Present, gift, reward	شكيب
Shākir	Thankful	شاكر

TRANSLITERATION	MEANING	NAME IN ARABIC
Shamāl	Wind that comes from the north	شمال
Shāmil	All comprehensive	شامل
Shamīm	Fragrant	شميم
Sharaf	Honor	شرف
Shumayl	Complete	شميل
Shams al Dīn	Sun of religion	شمس الدين
Sharīf	Honorable, noble	شريف
Shawqī	Affectionate	شوقي
Shihāb al Dīn	The star of religion	شهاب الدين
Shihād	Honey	شهاد
Shu'ayb/ Shu'aib	A prophet's name	شعيب
Shukrī	Thankfulness (deriv.)	شكري

TRANSLITERATION	MEANING	NAME IN ARABIC
Ṣā’ib	Appropriate, correct	صائب
Ṣabīḥ	Beautiful, pleasant, fond	صبيح
Ṣābir	Patient, persevering	صابر
Ṣabrī	Of patience, perseverance	صبري
Ṣādiq	Sincere, truthful	صادق
Ṣiddīq	Very truthful, upright	صدّيق
Ṣāfī	Pure, clear	صافي
Ṣafīy	Sincere friend	صفي
Ṣafīy al Dīn	Best friend of the faith	صفي الدين
Ṣafūḥ	Forgiving	صفوح
Ṣafwān	Solid rock, pure	صفوان
Ṣafwah/ Ṣafwat	The best, the chosen one	صفوة/ صفوت
Ṣāḥib	Companion	صاحب
Ṣakhr	Old Arabic name *(Lit.: Rock)*	صخر
Ṣalāḥ	Of Righteousness	صلاح

Transliteration	Meaning	Name in Arabic
Ṣalāḥ al Dīn	The righteousness of the faith *(Name of the Muslim leader who liberated Jerusalem from the Crusaders)*	صلاح الدين
Ṣāliḥ	Good, righteous *(A Prophet's name)*	صالح
Ṣaqr	Falcon	صقر
Ṣiddīq	Trusting, truthful	صدّيق
Ṣubḥī	Morning (deriv.)	صُبحي
Ṣuhayb/ Ṣuhaib	Red-haired *(Name of the first Roman to embrace Islam)*	صهيب

Transliteration	Meaning	Name in Arabic
Taḥsīn	Beautification	تحسين
Al Tāj	The crown	التاج
Taj al Dīn	Crown of the faith	تاج الدين
Tamīm	Strong, complete	تميم
Tāmir	Rich	تامر
Tammām	Perfection, strength	تمام

TRANSLITERATION	MEANING	NAME IN ARABIC
Taqīy	Devout, God-fearing	تقي
Taslīm	Submission	تسليم
Tawfīq	Success *(Granted by God)*	توفيق
Tawḥīd	Believing in One God	توحيد
Taysīr/ Taisīr	Facilitation *(Granted by God)*	تيسير
Thābit	Firm	ثابت
Thāmir	Fruitful, productive	ثامر
Thawāb	Reward	ثواب
Thawbān	Name of a companion of the Prophet	ثوبان
Taym/ Taim Allah	Servant of God	تيم الله

Ṭāhā	The two opening letters of Surah 20 of the Qur'an *(It is said to be one of the names of Prophet Muhammad)*	طه
Ṭāhir	Chaste, modest	طاهر

Transliteration	Meaning	Name in Arabic
Ṭalāl	Nice, admirable	طلال
Ṭalḥah	Kind of tree	طلحة
Ṭarafah	Old Arabic name *(Lit.: A kind of tree)*	طرفة
Ṭarīf	Rare, uncommon	طريف
Ṭāriq	Name of a star *(Qur'anic word)*	طارق

أسامة

Transliteration	Meaning	Name in Arabic
Ubay	Old Arabic name *(One with high self-esteem)*	أُبي
Umayyah	Old Arabic name of a famous tribe	أمية
Usāmah	Description of a lion	أسامة
Usayd/ Usaid	Cub, young lion	أُسيد
Usaym/ Usaim	Cub, young lion	أسيم
Uways/ Uwais	Old Arabic name, name of wolf	أويس
'Uday	Old Arabic name *(One who runs fast)*	عُديّ

Transliteration	Meaning	Name in Arabic
‘Ubaydah/ ‘Ubaidah	Servant of God	عبيده
‘Udayl/ ‘Udail	Old Arabic name	عُديل
‘Umar (Omer)	Old Arabic name, *(Name of the second caliph in Islam)*	عمر
‘Umayr/ ‘Umair	Old Arabic name *(Dimin. of ‘Umar)*	عمير
‘Uqbah	Name of one of the companions who conquered North Africa	عُقبة
‘Urwah	Old Arabic name, support, handle	عروة
‘Utbah	Old Arabic name	عُتبة
Uthāl	Name of a mountain	أثال
‘Uthmān	Old Arabic name *(Name of the third caliph in Islam)*	عثمان

Waḍḍāḥ	Bright, brilliant	وضاح
Wadī‘	Calm, peaceable	وديع
Wadīd	Favorable, devoted, fond	وديد
Wafīq	Successful	وفيق

TRANSLITERATION	MEANING	NAME IN ARABIC
Wahab	Giving	وَهَب
Wahhāb	To give, to donate *(One who donates a lot)*	وهاب
Waḥīd	Unique, single	وحيد
Wā'il	Old Arabic name, *(Also name of one of the companions of the Prophet)*	وائل
Wajdī	Of strong emotion, passion and love	وجدي
Wajīd	Smooth land	وجيد
Wajīh	Notable, distinguished	وجيه
Walīd	Newborn child	وليد
Walīf	Befriending	وليف
Walīy al Dīn	Supporter of the faith	ولي الدين
Walīy Allah	Supporter of God	ولي الله
Waqār	Dignity, sobriety	وقار
Waqqāṣ	Old Arabic name	وقاص
Ward	Blossoms, flowers	ورد
Waṣfī	Descriptive	وصفي
Wāṣīf	Describer	واصف
Wāṣil	Considerate, inseparable friend	واصل
Wasīm	Handsome, good-looking	وسيم

Transliteration	Meaning	Name in Arabic

ياسين

Yaḥyā	A Prophet's name *(Biblical John)*	يحيى
Yamān	Good tidings	يمان
Ya'qūb	A Prophet's name *(Biblical Jacob)*	يعقوب
Yasār	Wealth, comfort	يسار
Yāsīn	The two opening letters of Surah 36 in the Qur'an *(It is said to be one of the names of Prophet Muhammad)*	ياسين/ يس
Yāsir	Wealthy	ياسر
Yazan	Old Arabic name	يزن
Yazīd	To increase, enhance	يزيد
Yūnus	A prophet's name *(Biblical Jonah)*	يونس
Yusrī	Well-to-do, wealthy	يسري
Yūsuf	A prophet's name *(Biblical Joseph)*	يوسف

TRANSLITERATION	MEANING	NAME IN ARABIC
Zāhid	Abstentious, ascetic	زاهد
Zāhir	Bright, shining, flowery	زاهر
Zakī/ Zaky	Pure	زكي
Zaỵn al 'Ābidīn	The best of the worshippers	زين العابدين
Zayn al Dīn	Ornament of the religion	زين الدين
Zakarīyā	A prophet's name *(Biblical Zakaria)*	زكريا
Zakwān	Intuitive	زكوان
Zayd/ Zaid	Abundance	زيد
Zayn/ Zain	Beauty	زين
Ziyād	Super abundance	زياد
Al Zubayr/ Al Zubair	Strong, powerful, smart fellow	الزبير
Zuhayr/ Zuhair	Having flowers	زهير
Ẓafar	Victory	ظفر
Ẓāfir	Victorious	ظافر
Ẓahīr	Helper, supporter	ظهير
Ẓarīf	Nice, graceful, humorous	ظريف

Female Names

آمنة

Transliteration	Meaning	Name in Arabic
Ālā'/ Aalaa	Signs of Allah	آلاء
Āmāl	Hopes, aspirations	آمال
Āminah	Secure, *(Mother of the Prophet)*	آمنة
Āsiyah	Comforting, consoling *(Wife of Pharoah)*	آسية
Āyah	Qur'anic verse, clear evidence, sign of God	آية
Āyāt	Qur'anic verses, clear evidences, signs of God	آيات
Abrār	Devoted to God	أبرار
Adībah	Well-mannered, cultured, writer	أديبة
Afnān	Tree branches or twigs	أفنان
Afrāḥ	Celebrations, festivals	أفراح
Afyā'	Shadows	أفياء
Aḥlām	Dreams	أحلام
Almās	Diamond	الماس
Alṭāf	Kindness, politeness	ألطاف
Al Zahrā'	The illuminated *(Nickname of the Prophet's daughter Fāṭimah)*	الزهراء
Amal	Hope, aspiration	أمل
Amān	Security, peace, safety	أمان
Amānī	Wishes, aspirations	أماني
Amat Allah/Amatullah	Female servant of God	أمة الله
Amīnah	Trustworthy, faithful	أمينة
Amīrah	Princess, leader	أميرة

Transliteration	Meaning	Name in Arabic
Amjād	Magnificence, splendors	أمجاد
Anīsah	Friendly; of good company	أنيسة
Anjum	Stars	أنجم
Anmār	Old Arabic name, leopards	أنمار
Anwār	Rays of light, blossoms	أنوار
Ārām	Signs, flags	آرام
Arīj	Fragrance, sweet smell	أريج
Arwā	Female mountain goat	أروى
Aṣālah	Nobility of descent	أصالة
Ashwāq	Love *(Affections)*	أشواق
Asīl	Smooth	أسيل
Asīlah	Smooth	أسيلة
Aṣīlah	Noble origin, pure	أصيلة
Asmā'	Loftier, more eminent, *(Daughter of Abū Bakr, plural of Ism "name")*	أسماء
Asrā	Travel by night	أسرى
Asrār	Secrets	أسرار
Athīr	Favored, preferred	أثير
Aṭyāf	Fantasies	أطياف
Azhār	Flowers	أزهار

عبير

Transliteration	Meaning	Name in Arabic
'Abāl	Wild rose	عبال
'Ābidah	Worshipper	عابدة
'Abīr	Fragrance, perfume	عبير
'Ablah	Perfectly formed	عبلة
'Adawīyah	Summer's plant	عدوية
'Ādilah	Just, honest	عادلة
'Adīlah	Equal	عديلة
'Adn	Paradise	عَدْن
'Afāf	Chastity, modesty	عفاف
'Afīfah	Chaste, modest	عفيفة
'Afrā'	White	عفراء
'Ahd	Commitment, delegation, pledge	عهد
'Ā'idah	To return, to come back	عائدة
'Ā'ishah	Living, prosperous *(Wife of the Prophet)*	عائشة

Transliteration	Meaning	Name in Arabic
'Āliyah	Elevated, outstanding	عالية
'Alīyah	Exalted, highest social standing	علية
'Alyā'	Loftiness	علياء
'Anbar	Perfume *(Of ambergis)*	عنبر
'Anbarīn	Of ambergris	عنبرين
'Anān	Clouds	عنان
'Aqīlah	Wife, spouse, the best, the pick	عقيلة
'Arūb	Loving	عروب
'Āṣimah	Protector, capital	عاصمة
'Aṣmā'	Excellent	عصماء
'Aṣriyah	Modernist	عصرية
'Āṭifah	Affectionate, compassionate	عاطفة
'Ātikah	Pure, clear	عاتكة
'Aṭīyah	Gift, present	عطية
'Awāṭif	Emotions	عواطف
'Azīzah	Beloved, dear	عزيزة
'Azzah	Young gazelle	عزة

TRANSLITERATION	MEANING	NAME IN ARABIC
Badī‘ah	Astonishing, amazing	بديعة
Badrīyah	Resembling full moon	بدرية
Bahījah	Magnificent, splendid	بهيجة
Bahīrah	Dazzling, brilliant, noble lady	بهيرة
Bahiyah	Beautiful, radiant	بهية
Balqīs	Name of the Queen of Sheba	بلقيس
Balsam	Balsam, balm	بلسم
Bān	Kind of tree	بان
Banān	Fingertip	بنان
Barā’ah	Innocence	براءة
Barakah	Blessing	بركة
Bāri‘ah	Excelling	بارعة
Barīrah	Faithful and devoted	بريرة
Bashā'ir	Good news, good omens	بشائر
Bashīrah	Bringer of glad tidings	بشيرة
Bāsilah	Brave	باسلة

Transliteration	Meaning	Name in Arabic
Bāsimah	Smiling	باسمة
Basīmah	Smiling	بسيمة
Basīnah	Kitty, kitten	بسينة
Basmā'	Smiling	بسماء
Basmah	A smile	بسمة
Batūl	Virgin	بتول
Bayān	Clearness, eloquence	بيان
Baysān	To walk with pride	بَيْسان
Bisār	Adolescent	بسار
Budūr	Full moons	بدور
Buhaysah/ Buhaisah	Walking with pride	بُهيسة
Buhjah	Joy, delight	بُهجة
Buhthah	Happy, delighted when seeing others	بُهثة
Bushrā	Good omen, good news	بشرى
Busr	Unripe dates, star, height	بُسر
Buthaynah/ Buthainah	Beautiful and tender body	بثينة

دعاء

Transliteration	Meaning	Name in Arabic
Da‘d	Old Arabic name	دعد
Dalāl	Coquetry	دلال
Dāliyah	Grape vine, varix	دالية
Dāniyah	Closer, nearer	دانية
Dhākirah	One who remembers God frequently	ذاكرة
Dhakīyah	Bright, intelligent	ذكية
Dhukā'	Name of the sun	ذكاء
Dīmah	Cloud which carries rain	ديمة
Du‘ā’	Prayer, invocation (of God)	دعاء
Dunya	World	دنيا
Dunyānā	Our world	دنيانا
Durar	Pearls	دُرر
Durrah	Pearl	دُرّة
Durrīyah	Shining, bright	درية
Ḍuḥā	Forenoon	ضحى

فاطمة

Transliteration	Meaning	Name in Arabic
Fāḍilah	Outstanding	فاضلة
Faḍīlah	Virtue	فضيلة
Fādīyah	Redeemer, self-sacrifice	فادية
Fadwā	Name derived from self-sacrifice	فدوى
Fahīmah	Intelligent	فهيمة
Fā'iqah	Surpassing, excellent	فائقة
Fā'izah	Victorious, winner	فائزة
Fajr	Dawn, morning prayer	فجر
Fakhrīyah	Honorary	فخرية
Falak	Star	فلك
Fanan	Tree branch or twig	فنن
Faraḥ	Joy, cheerfulness	فرح
Farḥah	Lively	فرحة
Farḥānah	Happy	فرحانة
Farīdah	Unique	فريدة
Farīḥah	Happy, joyful	فريحة

Transliteration	Meaning	Name in Arabic
Farīzah	Arch, curb	فريزة
Fatḥīyah	Beginning	فتحية
Fāṭimah	Weaning *(Daughter of the Prophet)*	فاطمة
Fāṭin	Fascinating, captivating	فاتن
Fāṭinah	Fascinating, captivating	فاتنة
Fawz	Victory, success	فوز
Fawzah	Success	فوزة
Fawzīyah	Successful	فوزية
Fayḥā'	Fragrant	فيحاء
Fayrūz	Turquoise	فيروز
Fidā'	Redemption	فداء
Fiḍḍah	Silver	فضة
Fikrīyah	Intellectual	فكرية
Firdaws	Paradise, garden	فردوس
Firyāl	Old Arabic name	فريال
Furāt	Sweet (water)	فرات
Futūn	Fascinations	فتون

Transliteration	Meaning	Name in Arabic
Ghādah	Beautiful	غادة
Ghadīr	Stream, creek	غدير
Ghālīyah	Dear, beloved fragrant, expensive	غالية
Gharām	Love	غرام
Ghazal	Flirt, words of love	غزل
Ghazālah	(Female) gazelle	غزالة
Ghazwah	Military expedition	غزوة
Ghaydā'	Young and delicate	غيداء
Ghufrān	Forgiveness, pardon	غفران
Ghuṣūn	Branches	غصون
Ghunwah	Indispensable	غنوة
Ghunyah	Indispensable	غنية

Transliteration	Meaning	Name in Arabic

هاجر

Hadīl	To coo *(pigeon)*	هديل
Hādīyah	Guide to righteousness, calm	هادية
Hadīyah	Gift	هدية
Hafa	Light rain	هفا
Hājar	Wife of Prophet Ibrahim	هاجر
Hālah	Aureole	هالة
Ḥamdīyah	One who praises a lot	حمدية
Hanā'	Bliss, happiness	هناء
Hanādī	Proper name	هنادي
Hanī'ah	Of bliss, happiness	هنيئة
Hawādah	Pleasant	هواده
Hawāzin	Name of an Arabic tribe	هوازن
Hazār	Nightingale	هزار
Hayed	Movement, motion	هيد
Hayfā'	Slender, of beautiful body	هيفاء

TRANSLITERATION	MEANING	NAME IN ARABIC
Hayūd	A mountain, a place	هيود
Hibah	Gift, present	هبة
Hibat Allah	Gift of God	هبةالله
Hidāyah	Guidance	هداية
Hijrah	Migration *(Of the Prophet Muhammad from Makkah to Madinah)*	هجرة
Hind	Old Arabic name *(One hundred)*	هند
Hiyām	Love	هيام
Hudā	Right guidance	هدى
Hunaydah/Hunaidah	*(Diminutive of Hind)*	هنيدة
Hudūn	To become quiet	هدون
Hutūn	Clouds with rain	هتون
Huwaydah/ Huwaidah	Gentle	هويدة

Transliteration	Meaning	Name in Arabic
Ḥubāb	Aim, goal	حباب
Ḥabībah	Beloved	حبيبة
Ḥāfiẓah	Heedful, mindful	حافظة
Ḥafīẓah	Heedful, mindful	حفيظة
Ḥafṣah	Wife of the Prophet	حفصة
Ḥakīmah	Wise woman	حكيمة
Ḥalā	Sweetness	حلا
Ḥalīmah	Gentle, patient *(Prophet's nursing mother)*	حليمة
Ḥamīdah	Praise-worthy	حميدة
Ḥanān	Affectionate, loving, tender	حنان
Ḥanīfah	True believer	حنيفة
Ḥanīn	Longing, yearning	حنين
Ḥasnah	Beautiful	حسنة
Ḥasibah	Respected, noble	حسيبة
Ḥasnā'	Beautiful	حسناء
Ḥawā'	Eve	حواء
Ḥawrā'	Having eyes with a marked contrast of white and black	حوراء

Transliteration	Meaning	Name in Arabic
Ḥayāh / Ḥayāt	Life	حياة/ حيات
Ḥikmah/ Ḥikmat	Wisdom	حكمة/ حكمت
Ḥulyah	Jewel, ornament, finery	حلية
Ḥumayrā'/ Humaira'	Of reddish complexion *(Nickname the Prophet gave to his wife 'Ā'ishah)*	حميراء
Ḥūr	Virgins of paradise	حور
Ḥūrīyah	A Houri, virgin of paradise	حورية
Ḥusnā	Most beautiful	حسنى
Ḥusn	Beauty	حُسْن

Ibā'	Pride, sense	إباء
Ibtihāj	Joy, delight	إبتهاج
Ibtihāl	Supplication, prayer	ابتهال
Ibtisām	Smiling	ابتسام
Iftikār	Thinking, contemplation	افتكار
Iftikhār	Pride, vain, glory	افتخار
Īnās	Sociability	إيناس

Transliteration	Meaning	Name in Arabic
Īthār	Preference	إيثار
I'jāz	*(Inimitability of Qur'an)*	إعجاز
Ijlāl	Respect, honor	إجلال
Ikhlāṣ	Sincerity	إخلاص
Ikrām	Honor, hospitality	إكرام
Ilhām	Intuition	إلهام
Īmān	Faith, belief	إيمان
Imtithāl	Polite obedience	إمتثال
In'ām	Act of kindness, benefaction	إنعام
Inṣāf	Justice, equity	إنصاف
Intiṣār	Triumph	انتصار
Īsā'	Spacious, generous	إيساع
Is'ād	To bring happiness, to provide help	إسعاد
Is'āf	Relief, help	إسعاف
Isār	Fascinating	إسار
Ishrāq	Radiance, eradiation	إشراق
Ishfāq	Compassion, affection	إشفاق
Isrā'	Nocturnal journey *(Night journey of Prophet Muhammad from Makkah to Jerusalem)*	إسراء
Iṣṭilāḥ	Agreement	اصطلاح
I'tidāl	Straightness, tenseness	اعتدال
I'timād	Reliance, dependence	اعتماد

Transliteration	Meaning	Name in Arabic
Izdihār	Flourishing, blossoming	ازدهار

عزة

Transliteration	Meaning	Name in Arabic
‘Ibādah	Worship	عبادة
‘Idhār	Check, fluff	عذار
‘Iffah/ ‘Iffat	Chaste	عفة / عفت
‘Ināyah/ ‘Ināyat	Concern, care	عناية / عنايت
‘Iṣmah/ ‘Iṣmat	Purity, modesty, infallibility	عصمة / عصمت
‘Itāb	Censure	عتاب
‘Iṭāf	Clock	عطاف
‘Izzah	Might, power	عزة
‘Ulā	Upper, highest	عُلى

جمانة

TRANSLITERATION	MEANING	NAME IN ARABIC
Jābirah	Comforter *(To console)*	جابرة
Jadā	Gift, present	جدا
Jadwā	Gift, present	جدوى
Jalā'	Clarity, elucidation	جلاء
Jalīlah	Splendid, lofty	جليلة
Jamīlah	Beautiful	جميلة
Janā	Harvest	جنى
Janān	Heart, soul	جنان
Jannah	Garden, paradise	جنّة
Jawā	Passion, love	جوى
Jūn	Inlet, bay, gulf	جون
Jawnā'	The sun	جوناء
Jūnah	The sun	جونة
Juwān	Perfume	جوان
Jawāhir	Jewels	جواهر
Jawharah	Jewel	جوهرة

Transliteration	Meaning	Name in Arabic
Jawl	To move freely	جول
Jihān	Popular name, a river in Iran	جيهان
Jīlān	King's men, courtier	جيلان
Jinān	Gardens, paradise	جِنان
Jūd	Generosity	جود
Jūdī	Name of a mountain mentioned in the Qur'an	جودي
Juhānah	Young girl	جهانة
Juhaynah/ Juhainah	Name of an Arab tribe	جهينة
Jumān	Pearl	جمان
Jumānah	Silver pearl	جمانة
Juwayrīyah/ Juwairīyah	Wife of the Prophet	جويرية

TRANSLITERATION	MEANING	NAME IN ARABIC
Kāmilah	Complete, perfect	كاملة
Kamīlah	Perfect	كميلة
Karam	Generosity	كرم
Karawān	Variety of plover birds	كروان
Karīmah	Generous, noble	كريمة
Kawākib	Satellites	كواكب
Kawkab	Satellite	كوكب
Kawthar	River in Paradise	كوثر
Kifāḥ	Struggle	كفاح
Ḳhadījah	Wife of the Prophet	خديجة
Ḳhayrīyah	Charity, beneficence	خيرية
Ḳhālidah	Ever-lasting, immortal	خالدة
Ḳhāliṣah	Sincere, pure	خالصة
Ḳhawlah	A female deer	خولة

Transliteration	Meaning	Name in Arabic
Ḳhitām	Conclusion, termination	ختام
Ḳhulūd	Eternity, infinite, duration	خلود
Ḳulūṣ	Clearness, purity	خلوص
Ḳhuzāmā	Lavender	خزامى

Labībah	Sensible, intelligent	لبيبة
Lamā	Darkness of lips	لمى
Lāmi‘ah	Shine	لامعةٌ
Lamīs	Soft to the touch	لميس
Lamyā’	Dark-lipped	لمياء
Lānā	To be gentle, softer , tender	لانا
Laṭīfah	Kind, gentle	لطيفة
Lam‘ah	Brilliancy	لمعة
Lāzim	Essential, imperative	لازم
Layālī	Nights	ليالي
Layān	Gentle and soft	ليان
Laylā	Old Arabic name, rapture, elation	ليلى

Transliteration	Meaning	Name in Arabic
Līnah	Tender	لينة
Lubāb	The best part of a thing	لُباب
Lubābah	The innermost essence	لبابة
Lubān	Pine tree *(denotes long neck)*	لبان
Lubānah	Wish, desire	لبانة
Lublubah	Affectionate, tender	لبلبة
Lubnā	Kind of storax tree	لبنى
Lujā	Of great depth	لُجى
Lujayn/ Lujain	Silver	لجين
Lu'lu'	Pearls	لؤلؤ
Lu'lu'ah	A pearl	لؤلؤة
Lūnah	Date palm	لونة
Luṭfīyah	Delicate, graceful	لطفية

TRANSLITERATION	MEANING	NAME IN ARABIC

TRANSLITERATION	MEANING	NAME IN ARABIC
Ma'āb	A place to which one returns	مآب
Ma'ālī	Noble things	معالي
Madā	Utmost point, degree	مدى
Madīḥah	Praise, commendation	مديحة
Mafāz	Success, achievement, victory	مفاز
Mahā	Wild cow *(Has beautiful eyes)*	مها
Maḥabbah	Love, affection	محبة
Maḥāsin	Beauties	محاسن
Maḥbūbah	Beloved	محبوبة
Mahdīyah	Rightly guided	مهدية
Mahībah	Noble, respected	مهيبة
Mājidah	Glorious	ماجدة
Majīdah	Sublime	مجيدة
Makārim	Of good and honorable character	مكارم
Makkīyah	From Makkah	مكية

Transliteration	Meaning	Name in Arabic
Malādh	Protection, shelter	ملاذ
Malak	Angel	ملك
Malakah	Talent	ملكة
Malīḥa	Praising	مليحة
Malīkah	Queen	مليكة
Manāb	Deputyship, share	مناب
Manāl	Obtainment, attainment	منال
Manār	Guiding light *(Light house)*	منار
Marām	Aspiration	مرام
Mārīyah	Wife of the Prophet *(Lit.: fair complexion)*	مارية
Marzūqah	Blessed (by God), fortunate	مرزوقة
Marwah	A mountain in Makkah *(Al Safa wa al Marwah)*	مروة
Maryam	Mother of Prophet Jesus	مريم
Masarrah	Delight, joy	مسرة
Mas'ūdah	Fortunate	مسعودة
Mawaddah	Affection, love, friendliness	مودة
Mawāhib	Talents	مواهب
Māwīyah	Clear mirror	ماوية
May	Old Arabic name	مي
Maymūnah	Fortunate, blessed *(wife of the Prophet)*	ميمونة
Mays (mais)	Proud gait	ميس
Maysā'	Walking with pride	ميساء

Transliteration	Meaning	Name in Arabic
Maysam	Beautiful, stigma, brand	ميسم
Maysan	A star	ميسان
Maysarah	Left hand side	ميسرة
Maysūn	Walking with a proud, swinging gait	ميسون
Mayyādah	Walking with a swinging gait	ميادة
Mayyasah	Walking with a proud	مياسة
Mazāhir	Ancient Arabic variety of the lute	مزاهر
Minā	A place near Makkah	منى
Minnah	Kindness, grace, blessing	منّة
Mīrah	Provisions, supply	ميرة
Mu'azzaz	Powerful, strong	معزز
Mubīn	Clear, obvious	مبين
Mufīdah	Helpful, beneficial	مفيدة
Muḥibbah	Loving	محبة
Muhjah	Innermost, soul, heart	مهجة
Muḥsinah	Charitable, benevolent	محسنة
Mukarram	Honored	مكرم
Mukhliṣah	Devoted, faithful	مخلصة
Mumayyaz	Distinguished	مميز
Mu'minah	Faithful, believer	مؤمنة
Munā	Wish, desire	منى
Munawwar	Radiant, illuminated	منور

Transliteration	Meaning	Name in Arabic
Munīrah	Brilliant, illuminating	منيرة
Mu'nisah	Friendly	مؤنسة
Muntahā	The utmost, highest degree	منتهى
Murjānah	Small pearl	مرجانة
Murshidah	Guide	مرشدة
Murūj	Meadows	مروج
Mushīrah	Giving counsel, advising	مشيرة
Muṭī'ah	Obedient, compliant	مطيعة
Muzn	Rain, clouds	مُزن
Muznah	Rain, clouds	مزنة
Muyassar	Facilitated, wealthy, successful	ميسر
Muslimah	Submitting herself to God	مسلمة

TRANSLITERATION	MEANING	NAME IN ARABIC

نور

Nabīhah	Intelligent	نبيهة
Nabīlah	Noble	نبيلة
Nadā	Generosity, dew	ندى
Nađīdah	Equal, rival	نديدة
Nādirah	Rare	نادرة
Nādiyah	Announcement	نادية
Nadwah	Council, generosity	ندوة
Nafīsah	Precious	نفيسة
Nafla’	Surplus, overplus	نفلاء
Nāhid	One with full round breasts	ناهد
Nāhidah	One with full round breasts	ناهدة
Nahīdah	Big, huge	نهيدة
Nahlah	A drink (of water)	نهلة
Nā’ilah	Acquirer, obtainer	نائلة
Na‘īmah	Living a soft enjoyable life	نعيمة
Najāḥ	Success	نجاح
Najāt	Safety	نجاة

TRANSLITERATION	MEANING	NAME IN ARABIC
Najībah	Noble, distinguished	نجيبة
Nājīyah	Safe	ناجية
Najīyah	Safe	نجية
Najlā'	Of wide eyes	نجلاء
Najmah	Star	نجمة
Najwā	Confidential talk, romantic talk	نجوى
Narjis	Narcissus	نرجس
Nashwah	Fragrance, aroma	نشوة
Nasīm	Fresh air, breeze	نسيم
Nasmah	Breeze	نسمة
Nasrīn	Eglantier	نسرين
Nawāl	Gift	نوال
Nawār	One who dislikes bad deeds	نوار
Nazāhah	Purity, honesty	نزاهة
Nuḍār	Gold	نضار
Nawrah	Blossom, happiness, flower	نوْرة
Nawwār	May	نوّار
Nazīhah	Honest	نزيهة
Naẓīrah	Like-equal, matching	نظيرة
Nibāl	Arrows	نبال
Nibrās	Lamp, light	نبراس
Nīdā'	Call	نداء

Transliteration	Meaning	Name in Arabic
Nihād	Height	نهاد
Nihāl	Drink	نهال
Ni'mah	Blessing, loan	نعمة
Ni'māt	Blessings, loans	نعمات
Nisrīn	Kind of aromatic plant	نسرين
Niyāf	Tall and pretty	نياف
Nuhā	Mind, intelligence	نهى
Nujūd	Noble, wise	نجود
Nu'mā	Happiness	نُعمى
Namar	Name of a mountain	نمار
Nūnah	*(Lit.: dimple in the chin)*	نونة
Nūr	Light	نور
Nūr al Hudā	The light of the faith	نور الهدى
Nūrah	Corolla/ blossom	نورة
Nūrīyah	Radiant, brilliant	نورية
Nusaybah/ Nusaibah	Old Arabic name	نسيبة
Nuwayrah/ Nuwairah	Small fire	نويرة
Nuwwār	Blossoms, flowers	نوار
Nuwwārah	Blossom, flower	نُوارة
Nuzhah	Pleasure trip, promenade	نزهة

TRANSLITERATION	MEANING	NAME IN ARABIC
Qadr	Fate, destiny	قدر
Qadrīyah	To believe in God's will	قدرية
Qamar	Full moon	قمر
Qismah	Destiny, fate, *(Or ordained by God)*	قسمة
Qudsiyah	Glorious, sacred	قدسية

رحمة

Transliteration	Meaning	Name in Arabic
Rā'idah	Leader	رائدة
Ra'īfah	Merciful	رئيفة
Rabāb	White cloud	رباب
Rābi'ah	Fourth, Rābi'ah Al 'Adawīyah *(A famous Sufi woman)*	رابعة
Rabī'ah	Old Arabic name	ربيعة
Rābīyah	Hill	رابية
Rāḍīyah	Satisfied	راضية
Raḍīyah	Content, satisfied	رضية
Raḍwā	Name of mountain in Madinah	رضوى
Rafā'	Happiness, prosperity	رفاء
Rafāh	Pleasant, luxurious life	رفاه
Rafal	To trail a garment	رَفَل
Ra'fah/ Ra'fat	Mercy	رأفة / رأفت
Rafī'ah	Sublime, exquisite	رفيعة
Rāfidah	Support	رافدة

TRANSLITERATION	MEANING	NAME IN ARABIC
Rafīf	To gleam, shimmer	رفيف
Raghad	Pleasant	رغد
Raghdā'	Pleasant	رغداء
Rāghidah	Pleasant	راغدة
Rahā	Peaceful	رها
Rahaf	Delicate, fine	رهف
Raḥīmah	Merciful, compassionate	رحيمة
Raḥīq	Nectar	رحيق
Raḥmah	Mercy	رحمة
Rajā'	Hope	رجاء
Ramlah	Old Arabic name	رملة
Ramzīyah	Symbolic	رمزية
Ranā	To gaze, look	رنا
Rand	Laurel, sweet bay tree	رند
Randah	Tree of good scent	رنده
Ranīm	To recite in a singsong voice	رنيم
Rāniyah	Gazing	رانية
Rashā	Young gazelle	رشا
Rashad	Straight	رشد
Rashīdah	Wise, mature	رشيدة
Rasmīyah	Official, formal	رسمية
Raw'ah	Charm, beauty, splendor	روعة

TRANSLITERATION	MEANING	NAME IN ARABIC
Rawḍah	Garden	روضة
Rawḥah	Nice	روحة
Rawḥīyah	Spirituality	روحية
Rāwīah	Narrator, transmitter *(Of ancient Arabic poetry)*	راوية
Razān	Sensibility and respect	رزان
Rayḥānah	Aromatic sweet basil	ريحانة
Rayyā	Sated with drink	ريا
Riḥāb	Vastness, expanse	رحاب
Rihām	Lasting fine rain	رهام
Rīm	Gazelle	ريم
Rīmā	White antelope	ريما
Rimān	Name of place *(Dual of reem gazelle)*	ريمان
Ru'ā	Dreams, visions	رؤى
Rubādah	Ash-colored	رُبادة
Rukān	Steady, confident	ركان
Rubā	Hills, height	رُبى
Rudaynah/ Rudainah	Old Arabic name	ردينه
Rufaydah/ Rufaidah	Support, prop	رفيده
Rumaylah/ Rumailah	Old Arabic name	رُميلة
Rumaythah/ Rumaithah	Old Arabic name	رُميثة
Ruqayyah/ Ruqaiyah	Name of the Prophet's daughter	رقية
Rushd	Sensible conduct	رُشد
Ruwaydah/ Ruwaidah	Walking gently	رويده
Ru'yah	Dream, vision	رؤية

Transliteration	Meaning	Name in Arabic
Saba’	Sheba, name of town in Yemen	سبأ
Sadād	Right thing to do, lucky hand	سداد
Sa‘dah	Happy (happiness)	سعدة
Sa‘dīyah	Fortunate	سعدية
Saffānah	Pearl	سفّانه
Safūn	Breezing	سفون
Saḥar	Early dawn	سحر
Sahlah	Smooth, soft, fluent	سهلة
Sa‘īdah	Happy	سعيدة
Sajā	To be calm and quiet	سجى
Sājidah	Prostrating to God	ساجدة
Sakīnah	God-inspired peace of mind, tranquility *(Daughter of Alḥusayn ibn ‘Alī)*	سكينة
Sālimah	Safe, healthy	سالمة
Salīmah	Safe, healthy	سليمة
Salmā	Safe, healthy	سلمى

Transliteration	Meaning	Name in Arabic
Salsabīl	Spring in Jannah	سلسبيل
Salwā	Quail, solace	سلوى
Samāḥ	Generosity	سماح
Samar	Evening conversation	سمر
Samārah	Soft-light	سمارة
Samāwah	Summit, height	سماوة
Samīḥah	Generous	سميحة
Sāmirah	Entertaining companion	سامرة
Samīrah	Entertaining companion	سميرة
Sāmīyah	Elevated, lofty	سامية
Samrā'	Soft, light tanned color	سمراء
Sanā	Brilliance, splendor	سنا
Sanā'	Eminence, sublimity	سناء
Sanīyah	Resplendence, brilliance	سنية
Sārah	Wife of Prophet Ibrahīm	سارة
Sawdah	Proper name , wife of the Prophet	سوده
Sawsan	Lilly of the valley	سوسن
Sayyidah	Lady, woman, madam, mistress	سيدة
Sibāl	Eyes with long lashes	سبال
Sihām	Arrows	سهام
Sīmah	Sign, characteristic, expression	سيمة
Sirīn	Wife of Prophet's companion Ḥassān ibn Thābit	سيرين
Su'ād	Good fortune	سعاد

Transliteration	Meaning	Name in Arabic
Su'dā	Happy, luck	سعدى
Suhā	Name of star	سها
Suhaylah/ Suhailah	Smooth, soft, fluent	سهيلة
Suhaymah/ Suhaimah	Small arrow	سهيمة
Suhayr/ Suhair	Proper name	سهير
Sukaynah/ Sukainah	Charming, likable	سُكينة
Sulāfah	Choicest	سلافة
Sulṭanah	Sultaness	سلطانة
Sumayrā'/ Sumairā'	A name of place *(Diminutive of Samrā')*	سميراء
Sumayyah/ Sumaiyah	Proper name, name of a lady companion of the Prophet *(The first martyr in Islam)*	سمية
Sunbul	Spikes of grain	سنبل
Sunbulah	A spike of grain	سنبلة
Sundus	Silk brocade	سندس
Surā	To travel by night	سرى

Transliteration	Meaning	Name in Arabic
Shadan	A young gazille	شدن
Shadhā	Aroma	شذى
Shādhīyah	Aromatic	شاذية
Shādīyah	Singer	شادية
Shafīqah	Conpassionate, sympathetic	شفيقة
Shahd	Honey, honeycomb	شهد
Shahlah	Blush	شهلة
Shāhidah	Witness	شاهدة
Shahīrah	Well-known, famous	شهيرة
Shākirah	Thankful	شاكرة
Shāmilah	Complete, comprehensive	شاملة
Shams	Sun	شمس
Sharīfah	Honored, noble	شريفة
Shawq	Longing	شوق
Shaymā	To look out	شيماء

Transliteration	Meaning	Name in Arabic
Shifā’	Cure, healing	شفاء
Shīmah	Nature, habit	شيمة
Shiyam	Nature, characters	شيم
Shuhrah	Fame, reputation	شهرة
Shudūn	Power, straight	شدون
Shukrah	Thankfulness	شكران
Shukrīyah	Of thanks	شكرية
Shurūq	Rising, shining	شروق

Transliteration	Meaning	Name in Arabic
Ṣabā	A nice wind	صبا
Ṣbāh	Morning	صباح
Ṣabīḥah	Beautiful	صبيحة
Ṣābirah	Patient	صابرة
Ṣabr	Patience, self control	صبر
Ṣabrīyah	Patient	صبرية
Ṣafā	A hill in Makkah	صفا
Ṣafā	Clarity, purity	صفاء
Ṣafā'	Pure	صافية
Ṣāfiyah	Sincere friend (Wife of the Prophet)	صفية
Ṣfiyah	Righteous	صالحة
Ṣiddīqah	Upright, very truthful	صدّيقة
Ṣubḥah	In the morning	صبحة
Ṣbḥīyah	Of the morning	صبحية

Transliteration	Meaning	Name in Arabic
	تغريد	
Tabassum	Smiling	تبسم
Taghrīd	Singing, twitting	تغريد
Tahānī	Congratulations	تهاني
Taḥīyah	Greeting	تحية
Taḥīyāt	Greetings	تحيات
Tālah	Young palm tree	تاله
Tamāḍur	Brilliant	تماضر
Taqīyah	Heedful of God	تقية
Taqwā	Piety, devoutness, heedfullness of God	تقوى
Ta'sīyah	Consolation, comfort	تأسية
Tasnīm	Fountain in paradise	تسنيم
Tawbah	Repentence	توبة
Taymā'/ Taimā'	Oasis in NW Arabia	تيماء
Thanā'	Commendation, praise	ثناء
Tharā'	Wealth	ثراء
Tharwah	Wealth	ثروة
Thawāb	Reward	ثواب

Transliteration	Meaning	Name in Arabic
Thurayyā/ Thuraiyā	Star, Pleiades (A constellation)	ثريا
Tuqā	Heedfulness of God	تقى
Thuwaybah/ Thuwaibah	Name of female companion of the Prophet *(Lit.: Deserving of God's reward)*	ثويبة
Ṭāhirah	Pure, chaste	طاهرة
Ṭarūb	Merry	طروب
Ṭībah	Goodness, kindness	طيبة
Ṭūbā	Blessedness, beatitude	طوبى

'Ubāb	Waves, heavy rain	عباب
Ulfah	Harmony, intimacy	ألفة
Umāmah	Arabic name, the Prophet's granddaughter *(Lit.: Young mother)*	أمامة
Umaymah	Young mother	أميمة
Umm Kalthūm	Name of the daughter of Prophet Muḥammad	أم كلثوم

TRANSLITERATION	MEANING	NAME IN ARABIC
Umnīyah	A wish, an aspiration	أمنية
Usaymah/ Usaimah	Old Arabic name	أسيمة
‘Uhūd	Commitment, delegation, pledge	عهود
Uwaysah/ Uwaisah	Bilberry, whortleberry	أويسة

وعد

Wa‘d	Promise	وعد
Wadī‘ah	Calm, peaceable	وديعة
Waḍḥā	Bright	وضحى
Wafā’	Faithfulness	وفاء
Wafīqah	Successful	وفيقه
Wafīyah	Loyal, faithful	وفية
Wahbīyah	Giving	وهبية
Waḥīdah	Exclusive, unique	وحيدة
Wajd	Passion, strong emotion	وجد
Wajīhah	Eminent, notables	وجيهة
Walā’	Loyalty	ولاء

TRANSLITERATION	MEANING	NAME IN ARABIC
Wallādah	Frequently producing, off springs	ولادة
Wardah	Rose	وردة
Warqā'	Pigeon	ورقاء
Waṣfiyah	Depictive	وصفية
Wasīlah	Ingratiate	وسيلة
Wasīmah	Pretty, beautiful	وسيمة
Wi'ām	Harmony, agreement	وئام
Wid	Loving, affectionate	ود
Widād	Love, friendship	وداد
Wifāq	Harmony, consent	وفاق
Wijdān	Ecstasy, sentiment	وجدان
Wiṣāl	Reunion, being together	وصال
Wisām	Medal, badge of honor	وسام
Wurūd	Roses	ورود

Transliteration	Meaning	Name in Arabic

ياسمين

Yāminah	Blessed	يامنه
Yārah	Warm	يارة
Yāsamīn	Jasmine	ياسمين
Yumn	Good fortune, success	يمن
Yumna/ Yumnah	Right side	يمنى/ يمنه
Yusrā	Most prosperous	يسرى
Yusrīyah	Most prosperous	يسرية

زهراء

Transliteration	Meaning	Name in Arabic
Ẓāfirah	Victorious	ظافرة
Zāhidah	Ascetic, abstentious	زاهدة
Zāhirah	Shining, luminous	زاهرة
Zahīrah	Shining, luminous	زهيرة
Zakīyah	Pure	زكية
Zanūbīya	A great Syrian queen	زنوبيا
Zahrā'	White	زهراء
Zahrah	Flower, beauty	زهرة
Zahwah	Beauty, pretty	زهوة
Zaynab/ Zainab	Name of the Prophet's daughter *(Lit.: An ornamented tree)*	زينب
Zayn/ Zain	Beauty	زين
Zinah	Adornment, ornamentation	زينة
Zīnāt	Adornment, ornamentation	زينات
Zubaydah/ Zubaidah	Old Arabic name, *(Wife of Caliph Harūn Al Rashīd)*	زبيدة

Transliteration	Meaning	Name in Arabic
Zuhā	Adornment	زُها
Zuhrah	Brightness	زُهرة
Zuhūr	Flowers, to blossom, to glow	زهور
Zulaykhā/ Zulaikhā	The name of the wife of the Egyptian official who attempted to seduce Prophet Yusuf	زُليخا
Zumurrud	Emerald	زمرد